50 Pies & Tarts for Every Sweet Tooth

By: Kelly Johnson

Table of Contents

- Classic Apple Pie
- French Silk Pie
- Lemon Meringue Pie
- Pecan Pie
- Key Lime Pie
- Pumpkin Pie
- Cherry Pie
- Blueberry Pie
- Strawberry Rhubarb Pie
- Chocolate Ganache Tart
- Coconut Cream Pie
- Peanut Butter Pie
- Banana Cream Pie
- Blackberry Pie
- Raspberry Almond Tart
- Salted Caramel Pie
- Maple Walnut Pie
- Bourbon Chocolate Pecan Pie
- Cranberry Orange Tart
- Pear and Almond Tart
- Fig and Honey Tart
- Nutella Hazelnut Tart
- Passionfruit Meringue Pie
- S'mores Pie
- Chocolate Chip Cookie Pie
- Mocha Cream Pie
- Butterscotch Pie
- Sweet Potato Pie
- Black Forest Tart
- Pineapple Coconut Pie
- Chai Spiced Pear Pie
- Carrot Cake Pie
- Cinnamon Roll Pie
- White Chocolate Raspberry Tart
- Dulce de Leche Pie

- Almond Joy Pie
- Tiramisu Tart
- Matcha Green Tea Tart
- Apricot Frangipane Tart
- Grapefruit Custard Tart
- Honey Lavender Tart
- Espresso Brownie Pie
- Mango Coconut Tart
- Strawberry Basil Tart
- Chocolate Orange Tart
- Cherry Clafoutis Tart
- Plum and Thyme Tart
- Biscoff Cookie Butter Pie
- Pistachio Rose Tart
- Blackberry Lemon Tart

Classic Apple Pie

Ingredients:

For the crust:

- 2 ½ cups (315g) all-purpose flour
- 1 cup (226g) unsalted butter, chilled and cubed
- ½ teaspoon salt
- 1 tablespoon sugar
- 6-8 tablespoons ice water

For the filling:

- 6-7 medium apples (Granny Smith, Honeycrisp, or a mix), peeled, cored, and sliced
- ¾ cup (150g) granulated sugar
- ¼ cup (50g) brown sugar
- 1 teaspoon cinnamon
- ¼ teaspoon nutmeg
- ¼ teaspoon salt
- 1 tablespoon lemon juice
- 2 tablespoons cornstarch or all-purpose flour
- 1 tablespoon unsalted butter, cut into small pieces

For the topping:

- 1 egg, beaten (for egg wash)
- 1 tablespoon sugar (for sprinkling)

Instructions:

1. **Make the pie crust:**
    - In a large bowl, combine flour, sugar, and salt.
    - Add cold butter and use a pastry cutter or your fingers to mix until it resembles coarse crumbs.
    - Gradually add ice water, one tablespoon at a time, mixing until the dough comes together.
    - Divide into two disks, wrap in plastic wrap, and refrigerate for at least 1 hour.
2. **Prepare the filling:**

- In a large bowl, mix apple slices with sugars, cinnamon, nutmeg, salt, lemon juice, and cornstarch. Let sit for 15-20 minutes.
3. **Assemble the pie:**
    - Preheat oven to 375°F (190°C).
    - Roll out one dough disk on a floured surface and fit it into a 9-inch pie dish.
    - Pour apple filling into the crust and dot with butter pieces.
    - Roll out the second dough disk and place it over the apples. Seal and crimp the edges, then cut slits for steam to escape.
4. **Bake the pie:**
    - Brush the top crust with beaten egg and sprinkle with sugar.
    - Bake for 50-60 minutes, until golden brown and bubbly. If the edges brown too quickly, cover with foil.
5. **Cool and serve:**
    - Let the pie cool for at least 2 hours before slicing. Serve with vanilla ice cream or whipped cream.

French Silk Pie

Ingredients:

For the crust:

- 1 ½ cups (180g) graham cracker crumbs or chocolate cookie crumbs
- 6 tablespoons (85g) unsalted butter, melted
- ¼ cup (50g) sugar

For the filling:

- 4 ounces (113g) unsweetened chocolate, melted and cooled
- 1 cup (200g) granulated sugar
- ¾ cup (170g) unsalted butter, softened
- 1 teaspoon vanilla extract
- 3 large eggs

For the topping:

- 1 cup (240ml) heavy whipping cream
- 2 tablespoons powdered sugar
- Chocolate shavings (optional)

Instructions:

1. **Make the crust:** Mix crumbs, sugar, and melted butter. Press into a 9-inch pie dish. Chill for 30 minutes.
2. **Prepare the filling:** Beat butter and sugar until fluffy. Add melted chocolate and vanilla. Beat in eggs one at a time for 5 minutes each. Pour into the crust and refrigerate for 4+ hours.
3. **Make the topping:** Whip heavy cream with powdered sugar until stiff. Spread over pie and top with chocolate shavings.

Lemon Meringue Pie

Ingredients:

For the crust:

- 1 9-inch pie crust, pre-baked

For the lemon filling:

- 1 cup (200g) sugar
- 2 tablespoons cornstarch
- 2 tablespoons all-purpose flour
- 1 ½ cups (360ml) water
- 3 egg yolks
- ½ cup (120ml) lemon juice
- 1 tablespoon lemon zest
- 2 tablespoons butter

For the meringue:

- 3 egg whites
- ¼ teaspoon cream of tartar
- 6 tablespoons sugar

Instructions:

1. **Make the lemon filling:** Cook sugar, cornstarch, and flour in water until thick. Whisk in egg yolks, lemon juice, and zest. Add butter and pour into crust.
2. **Make the meringue:** Beat egg whites with cream of tartar until foamy. Gradually add sugar and beat until stiff.
3. **Assemble & bake:** Spread meringue over warm filling, sealing edges. Bake at 350°F (175°C) for 10-12 minutes. Cool and serve.

Pecan Pie

Ingredients:

For the crust:

- 1 9-inch pie crust, unbaked

For the filling:

- 1 cup (200g) brown sugar
- ½ cup (120ml) corn syrup (light or dark)
- ½ cup (120ml) maple syrup (or more corn syrup)
- 3 large eggs
- 4 tablespoons (57g) butter, melted
- 1 teaspoon vanilla extract
- ¼ teaspoon salt
- 1 ½ cups (180g) pecans

Instructions:

1. Preheat oven to 350°F (175°C).
2. Whisk sugar, syrups, eggs, butter, vanilla, and salt. Stir in pecans.
3. Pour into crust and bake for 50-60 minutes until center is set. Cover edges if they brown too fast.
4. Cool for 2 hours before slicing.

Key Lime Pie

Ingredients:

For the crust:

- 1 ½ cups (180g) graham cracker crumbs
- 6 tablespoons (85g) melted butter
- ¼ cup (50g) sugar

For the filling:

- 4 large egg yolks
- 1 can (14 oz) sweetened condensed milk
- ½ cup (120ml) fresh key lime juice
- 1 tablespoon lime zest

For the topping:

- 1 cup (240ml) heavy whipping cream
- 2 tablespoons powdered sugar

Instructions:

1. **Make the crust:** Mix ingredients, press into a 9-inch pie dish, and bake at 350°F (175°C) for 10 minutes. Cool.
2. **Make the filling:** Whisk yolks, condensed milk, lime juice, and zest. Pour into crust.
3. **Bake & chill:** Bake at 350°F (175°C) for 15 minutes. Cool, then chill for 3+ hours.
4. **Make the topping:** Whip cream with powdered sugar. Spread over pie before serving.

Pumpkin Pie

Ingredients:

- 1 unbaked 9-inch pie crust
- 1 can (15 oz) pumpkin puree
- ¾ cup (150g) brown sugar
- 1 teaspoon cinnamon
- ½ teaspoon ginger
- ¼ teaspoon nutmeg
- ¼ teaspoon cloves
- ½ teaspoon salt
- 3 large eggs
- 1 cup (240ml) heavy cream
- ½ cup (120ml) milk

Instructions:

1. Preheat oven to 375°F (190°C).
2. Whisk together pumpkin, sugar, spices, and salt.
3. Beat in eggs, then stir in cream and milk.
4. Pour into pie crust and bake for 50-60 minutes.
5. Cool completely and serve with whipped cream.

Cherry Pie

Ingredients:

- 1 double pie crust
- 4 cups (600g) fresh or frozen cherries, pitted
- ¾ cup (150g) sugar
- 3 tablespoons cornstarch
- 1 tablespoon lemon juice
- ½ teaspoon almond extract
- 1 tablespoon butter, cubed

Instructions:

1. Preheat oven to 375°F (190°C).
2. Mix cherries, sugar, cornstarch, lemon juice, and almond extract.
3. Pour into crust, dot with butter, and cover with top crust.
4. Brush with egg wash and cut vents.
5. Bake for 45-55 minutes. Cool before serving.

Blueberry Pie

Ingredients:

- 1 double pie crust
- 5 cups (750g) blueberries
- ¾ cup (150g) sugar
- ¼ cup (30g) cornstarch
- 1 tablespoon lemon juice
- 1 teaspoon cinnamon

Instructions:

1. Preheat oven to 375°F (190°C).
2. Mix blueberries, sugar, cornstarch, lemon juice, and cinnamon.
3. Pour into pie crust, add top crust, brush with egg wash.
4. Bake for 50-60 minutes until golden. Cool before serving.

Strawberry Rhubarb Pie

Ingredients:

- 1 double pie crust
- 3 cups strawberries, hulled and sliced
- 2 cups rhubarb, diced
- 1 cup (200g) sugar
- ¼ cup (30g) cornstarch
- 1 teaspoon vanilla extract

Instructions:

1. Preheat oven to 375°F (190°C).
2. Mix strawberries, rhubarb, sugar, cornstarch, and vanilla.
3. Pour into crust, top with lattice, and brush with egg wash.
4. Bake for 50-60 minutes. Cool before serving.

Chocolate Ganache Tart

Ingredients:

- 1 ½ cups (180g) graham cracker crumbs
- 6 tablespoons (85g) butter, melted
- 8 oz (225g) dark chocolate, chopped
- 1 cup (240ml) heavy cream
- 1 tablespoon butter

Instructions:

1. Preheat oven to 350°F (175°C). Mix crumbs and butter, press into a tart pan, and bake for 10 minutes.
2. Heat cream until steaming, then pour over chocolate. Let sit for 2 minutes, then whisk until smooth. Stir in butter.
3. Pour into crust and chill for 2+ hours.

Coconut Cream Pie

Ingredients:

- 1 baked 9-inch pie crust
- 2 cups (480ml) coconut milk
- ½ cup (100g) sugar
- 3 tablespoons cornstarch
- 3 egg yolks
- 1 teaspoon vanilla extract
- 1 cup (80g) shredded coconut

Instructions:

1. Heat coconut milk and sugar in a saucepan.
2. Whisk cornstarch with yolks, then slowly whisk in hot milk.
3. Cook until thick, then stir in vanilla and coconut.
4. Pour into crust and chill for 3 hours. Top with whipped cream.

Peanut Butter Pie

Ingredients:

- 1 graham cracker crust
- 1 cup (250g) peanut butter
- 8 oz (225g) cream cheese, softened
- 1 cup (120g) powdered sugar
- 1 cup (240ml) heavy cream, whipped

Instructions:

1. Beat peanut butter, cream cheese, and sugar.
2. Fold in whipped cream and pour into crust.
3. Chill for 3+ hours.

Banana Cream Pie

Ingredients:

- 1 baked 9-inch pie crust
- 2 cups (480ml) milk
- ½ cup (100g) sugar
- 3 tablespoons cornstarch
- 3 egg yolks
- 2 bananas, sliced
- 1 teaspoon vanilla extract

Instructions:

1. Heat milk and sugar. Whisk cornstarch with yolks and slowly mix in milk.
2. Cook until thick, then stir in vanilla.
3. Pour half into crust, layer with bananas, then top with the rest.
4. Chill for 3 hours and top with whipped cream.

Blackberry Pie

Ingredients:

- 1 double pie crust
- 4 cups (600g) blackberries
- ¾ cup (150g) sugar
- ¼ cup (30g) cornstarch
- 1 tablespoon lemon juice

Instructions:

1. Preheat oven to 375°F (190°C).
2. Mix blackberries, sugar, cornstarch, and lemon juice.
3. Pour into crust, add top crust, and brush with egg wash.
4. Bake for 50-60 minutes. Cool before serving.

Raspberry Almond Tart

Ingredients:

- 1 ½ cups (180g) almond flour
- ½ cup (65g) all-purpose flour
- ½ cup (100g) sugar
- ½ cup (113g) butter, softened
- 1 egg
- 1 teaspoon almond extract
- 1 cup raspberries

Instructions:

1. Preheat oven to 350°F (175°C).
2. Mix almond flour, all-purpose flour, sugar, and butter. Stir in egg and almond extract.
3. Press into a tart pan and bake for 15 minutes.
4. Top with raspberries and bake for 10 more minutes.

Salted Caramel Pie

Ingredients:

- 1 graham cracker crust
- 1 cup (200g) sugar
- ½ cup (120ml) heavy cream
- 4 tablespoons (57g) butter
- ½ teaspoon sea salt
- 1 cup (240ml) sweetened condensed milk

Instructions:

1. Heat sugar in a saucepan over medium heat until melted and amber-colored.
2. Stir in butter, then slowly add heavy cream. Stir in condensed milk and salt.
3. Pour into crust and chill for 4 hours.
4. Sprinkle with extra sea salt before serving.

Maple Walnut Pie

Ingredients:

- 1 unbaked 9-inch pie crust
- ¾ cup (180ml) maple syrup
- ½ cup (100g) brown sugar
- 3 eggs
- 4 tablespoons (57g) melted butter
- 1 teaspoon vanilla extract
- 1 ½ cups (180g) walnuts

Instructions:

1. Preheat oven to 350°F (175°C).
2. Whisk maple syrup, sugar, eggs, butter, and vanilla. Stir in walnuts.
3. Pour into pie crust and bake for 45-50 minutes.
4. Cool before serving.

Bourbon Chocolate Pecan Pie

Ingredients:

- 1 unbaked 9-inch pie crust
- 1 cup (200g) sugar
- ½ cup (120ml) corn syrup
- 3 eggs
- 2 tablespoons bourbon
- 4 tablespoons (57g) melted butter
- 1 cup (175g) chocolate chips
- 1 ½ cups (180g) pecans

Instructions:

1. Preheat oven to 350°F (175°C).
2. Whisk sugar, syrup, eggs, bourbon, and butter. Stir in chocolate and pecans.
3. Pour into crust and bake for 50-55 minutes.
4. Cool before serving.

Cranberry Orange Tart

Ingredients:

- 1 tart crust
- 2 cups (200g) cranberries
- ¾ cup (150g) sugar
- ½ cup (120ml) orange juice
- 1 tablespoon orange zest
- 2 tablespoons cornstarch

Instructions:

1. Preheat oven to 350°F (175°C).
2. Cook cranberries, sugar, juice, and zest until thick. Stir in cornstarch.
3. Pour into crust and bake for 15 minutes.
4. Cool before serving.

Pear and Almond Tart

Ingredients:

- 1 tart crust
- ½ cup (113g) butter
- ½ cup (100g) sugar
- 2 eggs
- 1 teaspoon almond extract
- ¾ cup (75g) almond flour
- 2 pears, sliced

Instructions:

1. Preheat oven to 350°F (175°C).
2. Beat butter and sugar, then add eggs and almond extract. Stir in almond flour.
3. Spread into crust and top with pears.
4. Bake for 35-40 minutes.

Fig and Honey Tart

Ingredients:

- 1 tart crust
- 8 oz (225g) cream cheese
- ¼ cup (60ml) honey
- 1 teaspoon vanilla extract
- 1 cup sliced figs

Instructions:

1. Preheat oven to 350°F (175°C).
2. Beat cream cheese, honey, and vanilla. Spread into crust.
3. Top with figs and bake for 15 minutes.
4. Drizzle with extra honey before serving.

Nutella Hazelnut Tart

Ingredients:

- 1 tart crust
- 1 cup (300g) Nutella
- ½ cup (120ml) heavy cream
- ½ teaspoon sea salt
- ½ cup (60g) chopped hazelnuts

Instructions:

1. Heat heavy cream and mix with Nutella. Stir in salt.
2. Pour into tart crust and chill for 3 hours.
3. Sprinkle with hazelnuts before serving.

Passionfruit Meringue Pie

Ingredients:

- 1 baked 9-inch pie crust
- 1 cup (240ml) passionfruit juice
- ¾ cup (150g) sugar
- 3 egg yolks
- 2 tablespoons cornstarch
- 3 egg whites
- ¼ teaspoon cream of tartar
- 6 tablespoons sugar

Instructions:

1. Cook passionfruit juice, sugar, yolks, and cornstarch until thick. Pour into crust.
2. Beat egg whites and cream of tartar until foamy. Slowly add sugar and beat until stiff.
3. Spread meringue over pie and bake at 350°F (175°C) for 10 minutes.

S'mores Pie

Ingredients:

- 1 graham cracker crust
- 1 ½ cups (260g) chocolate chips
- ¾ cup (180ml) heavy cream
- 2 cups mini marshmallows

Instructions:

1. Heat cream and pour over chocolate chips. Stir until smooth.
2. Pour into crust and chill for 3 hours.
3. Top with marshmallows and broil for 1-2 minutes until toasted.

Chocolate Chip Cookie Pie

Ingredients:

- 1 unbaked 9-inch pie crust
- ¾ cup (150g) brown sugar
- ½ cup (100g) sugar
- ¾ cup (170g) butter, melted
- 2 eggs
- 1 teaspoon vanilla extract
- 1 cup (120g) flour
- 1 cup (175g) chocolate chips
- ½ cup (60g) chopped walnuts (optional)

Instructions:

1. Preheat oven to 350°F (175°C).
2. Beat sugars, butter, eggs, and vanilla. Stir in flour, chocolate, and nuts.
3. Pour into crust and bake for 50-55 minutes.
4. Cool and serve with ice cream.

Mocha Cream Pie

Ingredients:

- 1 pre-baked 9-inch pie crust
- 1 cup (240ml) heavy cream
- ½ cup (120ml) brewed espresso, cooled
- ½ cup (100g) sugar
- ¼ cup (30g) cocoa powder
- 2 tablespoons cornstarch
- 3 egg yolks
- 4 oz (113g) dark chocolate, chopped
- 1 teaspoon vanilla extract
- Whipped cream and chocolate shavings for topping

Instructions:

1. Heat cream, espresso, sugar, cocoa, and cornstarch until thick.
2. Whisk in egg yolks and cook until smooth. Stir in chocolate and vanilla.
3. Pour into crust and chill for 3 hours.
4. Top with whipped cream and chocolate shavings.

Butterscotch Pie

Ingredients:

- 1 pre-baked 9-inch pie crust
- 1 cup (200g) brown sugar
- 3 tablespoons cornstarch
- 2 cups (480ml) milk
- 3 egg yolks
- 3 tablespoons butter
- 1 teaspoon vanilla extract

Instructions:

1. Cook brown sugar, cornstarch, and milk until thick.
2. Whisk in egg yolks and cook 2 minutes.
3. Stir in butter and vanilla, then pour into crust.
4. Chill for 4 hours before serving.

Sweet Potato Pie

Ingredients:

- 1 unbaked 9-inch pie crust
- 2 cups (450g) mashed sweet potatoes
- ¾ cup (150g) brown sugar
- ½ teaspoon cinnamon
- ¼ teaspoon nutmeg
- ¼ teaspoon salt
- 2 eggs
- ¾ cup (180ml) milk
- 4 tablespoons (57g) melted butter
- 1 teaspoon vanilla extract

Instructions:

1. Preheat oven to 375°F (190°C).
2. Whisk all ingredients and pour into crust.
3. Bake for 50-55 minutes. Cool before serving.

Black Forest Tart

Ingredients:

- 1 tart crust
- 1 cup (175g) chocolate chips
- ½ cup (120ml) heavy cream
- 2 cups (300g) cherries, pitted
- ¼ cup (50g) sugar
- 1 tablespoon cornstarch

Instructions:

1. Heat cream and mix with chocolate. Spread into crust.
2. Cook cherries, sugar, and cornstarch until thick.
3. Pour over chocolate and chill for 3 hours.

Pineapple Coconut Pie

Ingredients:

- 1 unbaked 9-inch pie crust
- 1 can (20 oz) crushed pineapple, drained
- ¾ cup (150g) sugar
- ½ cup (120ml) coconut milk
- 3 eggs
- 1 cup (80g) shredded coconut

Instructions:

1. Preheat oven to 375°F (190°C).
2. Mix ingredients and pour into crust.
3. Bake for 45-50 minutes. Cool before serving.

Chai Spiced Pear Pie

Ingredients:

- 1 double pie crust
- 3 pears, sliced
- ¾ cup (150g) sugar
- 1 teaspoon cinnamon
- ½ teaspoon cardamom
- ¼ teaspoon ginger
- ¼ teaspoon cloves
- 2 tablespoons cornstarch

Instructions:

1. Preheat oven to 375°F (190°C).
2. Toss pears with sugar, spices, and cornstarch.
3. Pour into crust, top with second crust, and bake for 50 minutes.

Carrot Cake Pie

Ingredients:

- 1 unbaked 9-inch pie crust
- 1 cup (120g) shredded carrots
- ¾ cup (150g) brown sugar
- ½ teaspoon cinnamon
- ¼ teaspoon nutmeg
- 2 eggs
- ¾ cup (180ml) heavy cream
- ½ teaspoon vanilla extract

Instructions:

1. Preheat oven to 350°F (175°C).
2. Mix all ingredients and pour into crust.
3. Bake for 50-55 minutes.

Cinnamon Roll Pie

Ingredients:

- 1 pie crust (or cinnamon roll dough)
- ¾ cup (150g) brown sugar
- 2 teaspoons cinnamon
- 4 tablespoons (57g) butter, melted
- 1 cup (120g) powdered sugar
- 2 tablespoons milk

Instructions:

1. Preheat oven to 375°F (190°C).
2. Spread butter, cinnamon, and sugar over dough. Roll and slice into swirls.
3. Arrange in pie dish and bake for 30 minutes.
4. Drizzle with icing.

White Chocolate Raspberry Tart

Ingredients:

- 1 tart crust
- 6 oz (170g) white chocolate, melted
- ½ cup (120ml) heavy cream
- 1 cup raspberries

Instructions:

1. Mix white chocolate with warm cream. Pour into crust.
2. Top with raspberries and chill for 2+ hours.

Dulce de Leche Pie

Ingredients:

- 1 graham cracker crust
- 1 can (14 oz) dulce de leche
- 1 cup (240ml) heavy cream
- 2 tablespoons sugar

Instructions:

1. Spread dulce de leche in crust.
2. Whip cream and sugar, then spread on top.
3. Chill for 3 hours.

Almond Joy Pie

Ingredients:

- 1 chocolate pie crust
- 1 cup (240ml) coconut milk
- ½ cup (100g) sugar
- 3 egg yolks
- 1 teaspoon vanilla extract
- 1 cup (80g) shredded coconut
- ½ cup (60g) chopped almonds
- 4 oz (113g) melted chocolate

Instructions:

1. Cook coconut milk, sugar, and yolks until thick. Stir in vanilla, coconut, and almonds.
2. Pour into crust, chill for 3 hours, then drizzle with melted chocolate.

Tiramisu Tart

Ingredients:

- 1 tart crust
- 8 oz (225g) mascarpone cheese
- ½ cup (60g) powdered sugar
- 1 cup (240ml) heavy cream
- ½ cup (120ml) brewed espresso
- 2 tablespoons cocoa powder

Instructions:

1. Whip mascarpone, sugar, and heavy cream.
2. Spread into crust. Brush espresso on top.
3. Dust with cocoa powder and chill for 3 hours.

Matcha Green Tea Tart

Ingredients:

For the crust:

- 1 ½ cups (180g) graham cracker crumbs
- 6 tablespoons (85g) butter, melted
- 2 tablespoons sugar

For the filling:

- 1 ½ cups (360ml) heavy cream
- ½ cup (120ml) whole milk
- ½ cup (100g) sugar
- 2 tablespoons matcha powder
- 3 egg yolks
- 1 teaspoon vanilla extract

Instructions:

1. Preheat oven to 350°F (175°C). Mix crust ingredients, press into a tart pan, and bake for 10 minutes.
2. Heat cream, milk, sugar, and matcha until warm. Whisk in yolks and vanilla, then cook until thick.
3. Pour into crust and chill for 3+ hours before serving.

Apricot Frangipane Tart

Ingredients:
For the crust:

- 1 ½ cups (190g) all-purpose flour
- ½ cup (113g) butter, chilled and cubed
- ¼ cup (50g) sugar
- 1 egg

For the frangipane filling:

- ½ cup (113g) butter, softened
- ½ cup (100g) sugar
- 1 cup (100g) almond flour
- 1 egg
- ½ teaspoon almond extract
- 4-5 fresh apricots, sliced

Instructions:

1. Preheat oven to 350°F (175°C). Mix crust ingredients, press into tart pan, and chill for 30 minutes.
2. Beat butter, sugar, almond flour, egg, and almond extract until creamy. Spread into crust.
3. Arrange apricots on top and bake for 35-40 minutes. Cool before serving.

Grapefruit Custard Tart

Ingredients:

For the crust:

- 1 ½ cups (190g) all-purpose flour
- ½ cup (113g) butter, chilled and cubed
- ¼ cup (50g) sugar
- 1 egg

For the custard filling:

- ¾ cup (180ml) grapefruit juice
- ½ cup (100g) sugar
- 2 egg yolks
- 2 tablespoons cornstarch
- 1 teaspoon vanilla extract

Instructions:

1. Preheat oven to 350°F (175°C). Mix crust ingredients, press into tart pan, and bake for 15 minutes.
2. Cook grapefruit juice, sugar, yolks, and cornstarch until thick. Stir in vanilla.
3. Pour into crust and chill for 2+ hours.

Honey Lavender Tart

Ingredients:

For the crust:

- 1 ½ cups (190g) all-purpose flour
- ½ cup (113g) butter, chilled and cubed
- ¼ cup (50g) sugar
- 1 egg

For the filling:

- 1 cup (240ml) heavy cream
- ¼ cup (60ml) honey
- 1 tablespoon dried lavender
- 2 egg yolks

Instructions:

1. Preheat oven to 350°F (175°C). Mix crust ingredients, press into tart pan, and bake for 15 minutes.
2. Heat cream, honey, and lavender. Let steep for 10 minutes, then strain.
3. Whisk in yolks and cook until thick. Pour into crust and chill for 3+ hours.

Espresso Brownie Pie

Ingredients:

For the crust:

- 1 chocolate cookie crust

For the brownie filling:

- ½ cup (113g) butter, melted
- 1 cup (200g) sugar
- ½ cup (60g) cocoa powder
- 2 eggs
- 1 teaspoon vanilla extract
- 2 tablespoons espresso powder
- ½ cup (60g) flour

Instructions:

1. Preheat oven to 350°F (175°C). Mix brownie ingredients and pour into crust.
2. Bake for 25-30 minutes until set.
3. Cool and serve with whipped cream.

Mango Coconut Tart

Ingredients:

For the crust:

- 1 ½ cups (190g) all-purpose flour
- ½ cup (113g) butter, chilled and cubed
- ¼ cup (50g) sugar
- 1 egg

For the filling:

- 1 cup (240ml) coconut milk
- ½ cup (100g) sugar
- 3 egg yolks
- 2 tablespoons cornstarch
- 1 cup diced mango

Instructions:

1. Preheat oven to 350°F (175°C). Mix crust ingredients, press into tart pan, and bake for 15 minutes.
2. Cook coconut milk, sugar, yolks, and cornstarch until thick. Stir in mango.
3. Pour into crust and chill for 3+ hours.

Strawberry Basil Tart

Ingredients:

For the crust:

- 1 ½ cups (190g) all-purpose flour
- ½ cup (113g) butter, chilled and cubed
- ¼ cup (50g) sugar
- 1 egg

For the filling:

- 1 cup (240ml) heavy cream
- ¼ cup (60ml) honey
- 1 teaspoon vanilla extract
- 1 tablespoon chopped fresh basil
- 1 cup sliced strawberries

Instructions:

1. Preheat oven to 350°F (175°C). Mix crust ingredients, press into tart pan, and bake for 15 minutes.
2. Heat cream, honey, and basil. Let steep for 10 minutes, then strain. Stir in vanilla.
3. Pour into crust and chill for 3+ hours. Top with strawberries before serving.

Chocolate Orange Tart

Ingredients:

For the crust:

- 1 ½ cups (180g) chocolate cookie crumbs
- 6 tablespoons (85g) butter, melted

For the filling:

- 6 oz (170g) dark chocolate, chopped
- ¾ cup (180ml) heavy cream
- ¼ cup (50g) sugar
- 2 tablespoons orange zest
- 2 tablespoons orange juice

Instructions:

1. Preheat oven to 350°F (175°C). Mix crust ingredients, press into tart pan, and bake for 10 minutes.
2. Heat cream, sugar, and orange zest. Pour over chocolate, let sit for 2 minutes, then stir until smooth. Mix in orange juice.
3. Pour into crust and chill for 3+ hours. Garnish with candied orange slices if desired.

Cherry Clafoutis Tart

Ingredients:

For the crust:

- 1 ½ cups (190g) all-purpose flour
- ½ cup (113g) butter, chilled and cubed
- ¼ cup (50g) sugar
- 1 egg

For the filling:

- 2 cups (300g) cherries, pitted
- ¾ cup (180ml) milk
- ½ cup (100g) sugar
- 3 eggs
- ½ cup (60g) flour
- 1 teaspoon vanilla extract

Instructions:

1. Preheat oven to 350°F (175°C). Mix crust ingredients, press into tart pan, and bake for 15 minutes.
2. Blend milk, sugar, eggs, flour, and vanilla until smooth.
3. Place cherries in crust, pour batter over them, and bake for 35-40 minutes.

Plum and Thyme Tart

Ingredients:

For the crust:

- 1 ½ cups (190g) all-purpose flour
- ½ cup (113g) butter, chilled and cubed
- ¼ cup (50g) sugar
- 1 egg

For the filling:

- 4 plums, sliced
- ¼ cup (50g) sugar
- 1 teaspoon fresh thyme
- 1 tablespoon cornstarch

Instructions:

1. Preheat oven to 375°F (190°C). Mix crust ingredients, press into tart pan, and bake for 15 minutes.
2. Toss plums with sugar, thyme, and cornstarch. Arrange in crust.
3. Bake for 30-35 minutes until golden.

Biscoff Cookie Butter Pie

Ingredients:

For the crust:

- 1 ½ cups (180g) Biscoff cookie crumbs
- 6 tablespoons (85g) butter, melted

For the filling:

- 1 cup (250g) Biscoff cookie butter
- 8 oz (225g) cream cheese, softened
- ½ cup (60g) powdered sugar
- 1 cup (240ml) heavy whipping cream

Instructions:

1. Preheat oven to 350°F (175°C). Mix crust ingredients, press into tart pan, and bake for 10 minutes.
2. Beat cookie butter, cream cheese, and powdered sugar.
3. Fold in whipped cream and pour into crust. Chill for 3+ hours.

Pistachio Rose Tart

Ingredients:

For the crust:

- 1 ½ cups (190g) all-purpose flour
- ½ cup (113g) butter, chilled and cubed
- ¼ cup (50g) sugar
- 1 egg

For the filling:

- 1 cup (240ml) heavy cream
- ½ cup (100g) sugar
- ½ cup (60g) pistachios, ground
- 2 tablespoons rose water

Instructions:

1. Preheat oven to 350°F (175°C). Mix crust ingredients, press into tart pan, and bake for 15 minutes.
2. Heat cream, sugar, pistachios, and rose water until thick.
3. Pour into crust and chill for 3+ hours.

Blackberry Lemon Tart

Ingredients:

For the crust:

- 1 ½ cups (190g) all-purpose flour
- ½ cup (113g) butter, chilled and cubed
- ¼ cup (50g) sugar
- 1 egg

For the filling:

- 1 cup (240ml) lemon juice
- ¾ cup (150g) sugar
- 3 egg yolks
- 2 tablespoons cornstarch
- 1 cup (150g) blackberries

Instructions:

1. Preheat oven to 350°F (175°C). Mix crust ingredients, press into tart pan, and bake for 15 minutes.
2. Cook lemon juice, sugar, yolks, and cornstarch until thick. Pour into crust.
3. Top with blackberries and chill for 2+ hours.

www.ingramcontent.com/pod-product-compliance
Lightning Source LLC
LaVergne TN
LVHW081327060526
838201LV00055B/2498